MONEYPOLY

Moyo Oluyinka CPA

DEDICATION

This book is dedicated to God first, for the strength, wisdom, and ability to produce this body of work. Secondly, I dedicate this book to my Family, for the support and early lessons in money management.

Lastly, this book is dedicated to anyone who seeks to understand and transform his or her financial life. Here is to becoming the financially confident YOU!

INTRODUCTION

They say money talks! So, have you ever wondered what YOUR money is saying? Is your money saying, "Yes! you're doing the thang! Put me to work" or is it saying "You're barely hanging. We need to do better"?

Each one of us has a relationship with money whether we would like to admit it or not. Think about it; if you feel confident in your ability to manage, utilize, and grow your money, then it is safe to assume that you have a good relationship with money. If you barely consider tracking money or do not consider it at all, it is safe to say that your relationship with money is not so great (Let's change that!).

GREAT NEWS! This book is here to help you have a better relationship with money. It is meant to be used extensively to help you:

1. Identify the current state of your relationship with money.

2. Develop better money habits (even if you consider your relationship to be good).

3. Develop and implement practical ways to make your money move and talk right.

This will be an interactive and engaging book, it will require your active participation as there are worksheets included in each chapter to help you visualize the points being made. Grab your favorite pen or pencil, and let's get to work! In portions where you are encouraged to participate and apply tips to your personal situation, you will see this icon:

To accomplish the three objectives set forth in this book, you need to know your money goals first.

Let's make some Money Moves, shall we?

Oh, one last thing, if you find any portion of this body of work insightful and would like to share, feel free to do so and give this work a shoutout using the hashtags

#MoneyTalks

#Moneypoly

#MoneypolyTips

#MoneyMoves

#MillenialMoney

#GenZFinance

#SecureTheBagSeries

CHAPTER 1

#MONEYGOALS

Every journey begins with a destination in mind. Before you can begin to use the tips or evaluate the effectiveness of the tips provided in this Moneypoly book, you must first ask yourself one important question:

"What are my financial goals?"

Below are some examples of financial goals to help you kickstart your brainstorming session.

- ✏️ Pay off student loans or other debts.
- ✏️ Save a specific amount of money by the end of the year.
- ✏️ Build an emergency fund (ideally to cover 6 -12 months of expenses).
- ✏️ Invest in the stock market, real estate, or cryptocurrency.
- ✏️ Build credit.

NOTE: You can save to achieve numbers 2 through 4, using this book. You will see how in more detail as you continue to read.

So, back to the question: "What are your financial goals?"

This question has many layers. To answer this one important question, you will need to take a few moments to answer a series of other questions. My hope is that you can identify exactly what matters most to you in your financial life. Grab your pencil/pen and let's answer the following questions using the worksheet provided.

Where do you see yourself financially in the short-term (<1 YEAR) and long-term (>1 year)?

How much would you like to have in your checking, savings, and retirement accounts? How much would you like to save annually?

In the T-Chart below, write out your short-term goals and long-term goals on the left side.

To the right side of the T chart, rate how critical each of these goals are.

1= Not critical, 2= Somewhat critical, 3= Neutral, 4= Critical, 5= Extremely Critical

Pick your top goals (rated 5), one from the short-term section and one from the long-term section, and write out simple steps you can take, starting today, that can help you achieve those goals.

Short and Long Term Goals Worksheet

Short and Long Term Goals Worksheet

Long-Term Goals < 1 Year	Rating

Long-Term Goals < 1 Year

Let's use this example, if your short-term goal is to save $10,000 over a year, then one simple step would be to calculate how much you need to save monthly. You can then drill-down to how much you need to save weekly or maybe even daily if you really want to get aggressive with pursuing your goals.

To compute how much you need to save monthly, divide your total savings goal amount by 12 since there are 12 months in a year. $10,000/12 = $833.33/month. This means that you will need to save about $833 every month to meet your $10,000 in a year savings goal. If you would like to take this further, you can compute the weekly contribution by dividing $833 by 4. So, to save $10,000 within one year, you need to save $208 every week. Another simple step would be to start saving that amount either weekly or monthly.

Alright, take a moment to complete the worksheet and write out simple steps for each goal starting with the highest rated goals until you get to the lowest rated items (rated 1).

■■

Now that you have completed the worksheet with your short-term and long-term goals, let us discuss your income and your motive for saving, if you are already doing that.

Short and Long Term Goals Worksheet

Goals ranked 5:

____

____

____

____

____

____

____

____

____

____

____

____

Short and Long Term Goals Worksheet

Goals ranked 4:

Short and Long Term Goals Worksheet

Goals ranked 3:

Short and Long Term Goals Worksheet

Goals ranked 2:

Short and Long Term Goals Worksheet

Goals ranked 1:

To be sure that your financial goals are reasonable and within your ability, you must be honest about your income. Here is a question that should help you get clear on your income.

How much is your weekly income? - Consider whether you get paid weekly or bi-weekly.

If you get paid once a month, divide your monthly income by 4. On average, there are 4 weeks in a month.

If you receive a paycheck every other week, you get paid bi- weekly. Divide your bi-weekly income by 2. This will give you your weekly income.

If you get paid every week, well this is the number you would use as your weekly income.

Do you have your magic Number? Good.

Now let us discuss how you currently use your income. In other words, what happens once that check hits? Cha-Ching!

Income Allocation

How do you currently allocate your income? An example of income allocation is the **50/30/20 allocation** toward monthly expenses, savings, and investments. In other words, 50% of your income covers monthly expenses and benevolence fund, 30% of your income is allocated to savings, and 20% is allocated to investments.

NOTE: This allocation assumes that miscellaneous expenses such as shopping and self-care are included in the monthly expenses. If you currently do not know how your income is allocated among your expenses and other avenues, do not worry, you will get a chance to identify this in Chapter 4. For now, list out everything you spend or use money for. Write out the amounts you pay for each expense monthly, add them together, and divide that total by your monthly net income. Got the number? Multiply it by 100, this is your monthly expense allocation.

Savings Goal

Why are you saving? Notice that I did not ask whether you are saving or not, because a key action anyone should take is to save. You work hard to support yourself; a great way to reward yourself is to pay yourself first! Most financial advisors and coaches will suggest paying off your debt first before you start saving; however, I believe that it is best to put some funds aside. Save to build an emergency fund for example. It may seem like an impossible ordeal to save money when what you currently have is barely meeting your current needs, but trust me when I say the hardest step to take is the first step. You can start saving as little as $25. We will discuss easy ways you can do this in Chapter 3. For now, let us get back to the question: How much are you saving? Or if you are not, why would you like to save?

So, let's figure out reasons you would like to save:

1. Build an emergency fund: An emergency fund is a bank account, preferably a savings account, in which money is set aside to cover unexpected expenses. Financial advisors encourage saving enough to cover up to 3-6 months of living expenses, unforeseen repairs, or medical expenses. According to Suze Orman, the average person should have savings that can cover 12 months of your living costs*(1)*.

Before you get overwhelmed by this goal, I want to encourage you that this is a goal that is achievable over time. It is never too late to get started! I started my savings account with a whopping $25! I initiated a direct deposit into a savings account I opened a month prior to setting up the direct deposit.

So, every pay period, a deposit of $25 went into my savings before I even got paid. Multiply $25 by 2 (for bi-weekly pay) and then by 12 (for 12 months in a year), that is a total of $600 saved without me thinking about it. That may not seem like a lot of money, but do that over a 3-year period and you have $1,800 saved up, without considering compound interest. You do not have to start at $25, you can begin with $10, $20, $50 or $100.

■■

If you currently do not have an emergency fund, you are living life on the edge. Hey Daredevil! Let's create a safety net for when life hits because it is inevitable. Setting up a budget can help you see the bigger picture of how your money currently moves.

In fact, in chapter 2, we will determine your money profile; this will help to identify your money's current journey and ways you can adjust your money habits to better improve how your money moves.

Monthly Expenses Worksheet

Monthly Expenses	Amount
TOTAL (sum):	
ALLOCATION (sum/net income)*100:	%

In the meantime, to identify how much you need in your emergency fund, list out all your monthly expenses and multiply that total by 12 months. This is the total amount you need to have in your emergency fund savings account.

In Chapter 4, we will dive deeper into the "how" of budgeting; here you will detail your monthly income and expenses.

2. **Investment fund:** Unless you have been living under the rock over the last 10+ years, you have heard a thing or two about investing. Be it investing in real estate, the Stock market, or Cryptocurrency.

According to Dave Ramsey(2), you are better off waiting until you are debt-free and have six months of expenses saved in an emergency fund before you decide to start investing. I agree about the emergency funds part of that statement, which is why investing comes after building an emergency fund. If you have debt, you can still save and invest. You would simply need to tighten up your budget. If you are debt free…**CONGRATULATIONS!** You can save funds you intend to invest.

Now, you may be wondering "why would I save to then invest?" One reason is that if you do not need the money within the next 5 years, you may be better off investing, rather than keeping them in a savings account. The rate of return in the market is likely higher than that of a savings account; however, I must note that the risk is higher with investing. You can earn as high as 2% in interest annually in a High Yield Savings account, whereas you can earn as high as 9% annually from investing in the stock market. According to

Goldman Sachs, the average stock market return for 10 years is 9.2%. On the other hand, in 2018, S&P 500 annual return was -4.4% loss(*3*). You can lose money while investing in the stock market. We will discuss more on investing in another edition of **Moneypoly**. Invest now, enjoy later.

3. **Benevolence Fund:** Simply put, benevolence is an act of kindness. If you have a principle of being kind by giving to others who are less privy to having funds readily available, you can decide to save some money solely to assist anyone who you identify needs financial support. Personally, I have a separate bank account in which I save funds I intend to use to buy gifts or to give anyone in need. You will have to decide for yourself exactly how much you would like to save on a weekly or monthly basis. I save 10% of my paycheck for this purpose.

4. **Wedding/Car/House/TravelNoire funds:**
I understand that not everyone desires to get married, so I have suggested other options here like saving money for the down payment to purchase a car, a house or jet set! Ultimately, the main point is that you have something big you are saving for and exactly how much you need to save. Keep in mind, you do not need to limit your total savings to that specific amount; however, you will need to save the amount needed at a minimum.

5. **Pay off debt:** Majority of the population has one form of debt or the other. Forms of debt range from that cute credit card you got from your favorite store, to a 30-year Mortgage on that fancy home (although, this is more of an investment than debt. We will delve into this in another edition of **Moneypoly**.

According to Bankrate, as of November 2020, consumer debt was at $14.2 trillion…you read correctly…***TRILLION!!****(4)* Experian reported that as of 2019, about 14 percent of U.S. adults are burdened with student debt. Experian also identified that 90 percent of U.S. adults have at least one credit card, and about 75 percent of adults carry a balance from month to month. Nearly 25 percent of U.S. adults have personal loan debt. Debt will be covered in more detail in the next edition of Moneypoly. For now, here is a #protip:

If you desire to pay down your debt, you can save up some funds to pay it down. If you have no debt, congratulations! You can save toward other initiatives and put your money to work for you!

While I am a strong proponent of saving, investing, and setting up your future as best as you can, I would also advise that you be careful not to neglect your personal needs and forget to live in the present moment as tomorrow is only hoped for not necessarily promised. Live life wisely.

Now that you have an idea of why you are saving or why you would like to start saving, it is appropriate to understand your current relationship with money and money moves. I am a firm believer that to know where you are going, you must first understand where you have been and where you are. A solid financial understanding makes for a great foundation for strong financial health and literacy.

CHAPTER 2

MONEY PROFILES

WHERE IS MY MONEY?!

This section is designed to help you identify what I call your **Money Profile**. Most of us fall under one of these categories we will define further. For now, my question to you is: are you currently a Checkmate, a Savestake, a Spendinista, an Investomaster, or a MoverNShaker?

Understanding your money profile will also help you identify where your Money begins and ends its journey.

Meet the Money Profiles

Checkmate: Are all your monies sitting in a checking account? In other words, is the only bank account you have a checking account at your Local or National bank? If your answer is "yes," you, dear friend are what I call a Checkmate. While there is nothing wrong with having a checking account, the reality of the matter is that your money is not working for you in any way. In fact, it is wasting away as days go by and as expenses come up.

SaveStake: Do you have a savings account in addition to a checking account? What type of Savings account do you have? Is it a high yield savings account or a traditional regular savings account? Do you know the Annual yield on this savings account?

I'll share different types of savings accounts further in this chapter. For now, if you do have any type of savings account, you are what I call a SaveStake. If you do not and have a means of generating income, there is no reason you should not have a savings account. Refer to Chapter 1 for reasons to save.

Spendinista: Does your money barely spend its time in either of the accounts listed above? Are you actively churning out funds from your checking and saving accounts into expenses? Can't afford to miss out on that next TavelNoire experience, even though you know you can't afford to? If this is a yes for you, you are a Spendinista extraordinaire.

Trust me, I am a recovering shopaholic, so I definitely understand the struggle to say "NO". Those gorgeous pair of shoes whisper your name as you walk by, or is it that flourishing rare Monstera plant that calls out to your heart? I get it! But ask yourself this question: "How are these generating more funds for me?" Remember, the goal is to make your money say "You're doing the thang. Put me to work!"

InvestoMaster: Do you put some of your money to work in the money market or stock market somehow? Do you have an active 401k account, Health Savings Account (HSA), Traditional IRA, or Roth IRA set up? Are you in on the Crypto wave? If you have at least one of these accounts, you are an InvestoMaster.

MoverNShaker: Do you fall into more than one of the pro- files listed above? Do you feel that you have a good balance between all 4 money profiles? You, dear friend, are what I call a MoverNShaker. You are making money moves that will benefit you tremendously both now and in the future. Keep up the great work!

After reading the description of each money profile, I am almost certain that you do not need a questionnaire to help you identify which profile best describes you. We all know our current money habits and whether we could use some more help in certain areas or not.

For me, I was a Spendinista for a very long time. I simply enjoyed retail therapy; I mean who doesn't love stylish clothes and shoes?! It took some work to rebalance my relationship with money, but thankfully I believe that I am now on the right track and heading in a good direction. I am happy to say I am currently an InvestoMaster, working my way to becoming a MoverNShaker. I would like you to join me!

My goal is not to make you feel bad about your habits, but to enlighten you and make you do better as far as your money habits. Remember, the goal is to have your money talking and moving right!

There are at least 4 moves that money makes for every individual on the face on this Earth. When you read any finance literature, whether it is an article, a blog post, a book, or even a quick meme, you will notice that most of these follow a standard format/fact pattern. In fact, if you paid close attention to the money profiles, you would notice the same pattern.

Standard Money Move Model®

Where does your money begin and end its journey? Keeping your money profile in mind, let's work through the money model. The Money move model is essentially the series of steps that money takes, from generating it to spending or growing it.

Notice that the money move model is a three-legged model, if you"re a nerd like me, you notice the triangles within the three-dimensional pyramid.

Money Move Model

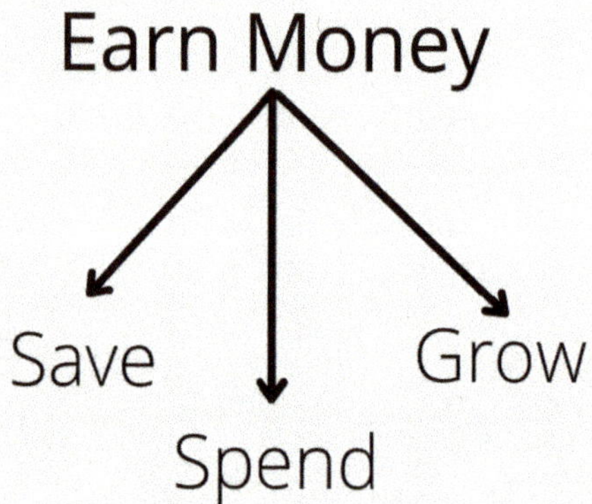

This is a three-legged model. The best way for this model to remain well-balanced is if all three legs are in use. If only 2 of the three legs are used, the model would be off-balance.

Essentially, your money moves model would be off-balance and before you know it, your money moves are headed for a disastrous destination. Picture this money move; you earn money and then decide to only save and spend, no investing. The risk in this off-balance journey is that by the time you have exhausted your "spend" portion, you are only left with your "save" portion.

After you have spent part of your earnings and need to cover some more expenses, guess where you would have to dip into? Yup, that's right- your savings. Before you know it, this will become a habit over time, and *POOF* goes your saved portion.

1. **Make Money: 9-5, Business, Side hustles, e.t.c:** This is the first step in the money move model, because this is the way we generate money. Whether you currently have a 9-5 job or are an entrepreneur who runs your business full time or currently as a side hustle, money finds its way into your possession from one of these legitimate sources. If by any chance you illegitimately source your current funds, consider doing the right thing.

> **Side note:** A current practice in our culture that demonizes and stigmatizes the general population who make their earnings from working a 9-5 job. It makes me wonder what we think about our parents who supported and provided for us by working these same 9-5 jobs we demonize. Do we consider our parents "less than", simply because they woke up and chose to go into an institution or establishment to work for 8 hours a day? It is concerning that our generation/culture has an issue with this method of making an income. Think about that phone number you called to have your business internet troubleshooted, do you think that would have been possible if someone was not working that 9-5 job? NO.

So, dear reader, whether you currently have a 9-5 job or are an entrepreneur who run your business full time or currently as a side hustle, if you are making your money legitimately, keep it up!

2. **Save Money:** You may wonder, "Why should I have a savings account? I already have a checking account." There are several benefits to having a savings account. For one, it will help with establishing an emergency fund and travel funds (#TravelNoireFunds) as we discussed in Chapter 1. It will also help to generate passive income by way of paying you interest on your savings. When deciding which type of savings account you would like to open, there are many options and criteria to consider. Savings account options include **Traditional savings Account, High Yield Savings Account, and Certificate of Deposit**(5).

- **Traditional savings accounts** are saving accounts you will find at your traditional commercial banks; think Bank of America, Chase, Wells Fargo, e.t.c.

  You can earn interest on your money, although the rates are very low.

- **High yield savings accounts** are just that; you can earn higher interest than you would from a regular savings account since they offer higher Annual percentage Yield (APY).

- **Certificate of Deposit** is another form of savings account with competitive APY; your money earns interest; however, the money must stay locked in the account for a specific period. Early withdrawal from a Certificate of Deposit account will trigger a withdrawal penalty, but if cash liquidity is important to you, there are some 3-month CD accounts.

Generally, the questions many ask are "How do I compare regular savings accounts to high yield savings accounts?" "What criteria should I consider?" Today is your lucky day! Below is a table that details some critical criteria to consider when deciding on the type of savings account to open. Feel free to use this and share it with anyone you think could benefit from this. #MoneypolyTips

🔍 Let's compare Savings Accounts

Criteria	Definition
Annual Percentage Yield (APY)	This is the annual rate at which your funds grow compounded.*
Minimum deposit requirement	This is the amount you must have in order to open up an account.
Minimum balance requirement	This is the lowest balance to have in the account at any given period. Any less, and you will be charged a maintenance fee .
Maintenance Fee	This is a fee banks charge for maintaining your account. Not all banks charge maintenance fees.

***Rule of 72: Divide 72 by the stated APY on an account. This will give you the number of years it will take for your funds to double if you do not add any more funds.**

Let's compare Savings Accounts

Criteria	Definition
Ease of Deposit	Confirm if you can easily deposit funds into this account and can link external accounts.
Ease of Withdrawal	This is how easily you can withdraw funds from the account and how long it take to withdraw funds.
Withdrawal Limit	Identify if there are limits to the number of withdrawals allowed per month.
Withdrawal Penalty	This is a fee you will be charged if you exceed the monthly withdrawal limit.

Once you have reviewed and answered each of the 8 points listed in the tables above for each type of savings account previously mentioned, you should have a better understanding of which you would like to utilize. Note that the option for you would be the option that retains as much of your money in the account as possible. You do not want to open an account that could rob you of your hard-earned money if you can help it!

3. Spend Money: One question that most people ask after reviewing their bank account is "Where is all my money going?!" Everyone has one expense or the other that needs to be paid, unless you are an heir of a wealthy family. A great way to answer that question is to track your spending and start budgeting. You created a monthly expense list in chapter 1; I hope that exercise allowed you to identify areas that demand a large portion of your funds. After you have covered your monthly expenses and met your financial obligations, if you still have some funds to use, the next best thing to do is to put those funds to work.

4. Grow Money: Let's face it, our goal in life is no longer just to make money, it is to build sustainable growth in money a.k.a WEALTH. Ultimately, everyone's goal is, or should be to maximize income, getting a lot more use for their funds. Essentially, we all want to be **MoversNShakers**. There are methods and ways to generate and establish a continuous flow of money. The methods are but not limited to Work, Business, and Passive income streams, like investing. This leg of the money move model focuses on increasing and growing money you primarily generate from your work or business, and a surefire way to do that is through investing. In Chapter 1, I shared the average return over the last few years. Over the last 10 years, the stock market has had a return of 9.2%3. As mentioned in previous chapters, there are many ways to participate in investing, and these methods will be discussed more in the next series of **Moneypoly**. For now, here are some common and easy methods that can be implemented today.

A. Real Estate

B. Invest by using:

- 401k account

- Dividend generating Index funds

- Foreign Currency Exchange

- Purchasing Life insurance.

Make contributions to either your 401k, your IRA, or any other investment portfolio you may have. In the second series of **Moneypoly**, we will dive deeper into investments.

Remember, the objective is to make money moves that will put your money to work and ultimately grow money.

5. Repeat!: The money model helped me to learn how to manage my finances better. So far, the process of splitting funds between saving, spending, and investing the remainder has been working well for me. if you are currently unsure about anything addressed here, feel free to reach out with questions and prepare yourself to be dazzled by the next book.

The best way for the money move model to remain well balanced is if all three legs are in use simultaneously. If only 2 of the three legs are used, the model would be off-balance.

Picture this money move; you earn money and then decide to only save and spend, no investing. The risk in this off-balance journey is that by the time you have exhausted your "spend" portion, you are only left with your "save" portion.

After you have spent part of your earnings and need to cover some more expenses, guess where you would have to dip into? Yup, that's right- your savings. Before you know it, this will become a habit over time, and *POOF* goes your saved portion. Think back to your identified money profile and assess your money moves based on the model presented above. Is your current model well balanced?

Now that you have identified your money profile and understand the money move model, you are able to hone in on the next best steps for you on your MoneyMoves journey.

CHAPTER 3
PAY YOU! SAVES-TAKE

Saving is the preservation of money for future use. Many will likely suggest budgeting before you begin to save. However, I believe that a better approach is to Pay yourself first!

Save some money, build your emergency fund, and then budget for your monthly expenses and obligations. You are doing all the hard work to earn the money, why wouldn't you pay yourself first? Paying for your living expenses is not you paying yourself; let no one convince you of that. I have found that saving teaches discipline.

When we have less money to work with, we are more inclined to think solely about necessities rather than wants. In turn, your budget becomes more needs based than it would, without the financial constraints. Therefore, I believe it is more important to pay yourself first before creating a budget.

I cannot stress how critical it is to have at least one savings account. As discussed in chapter 1, there are many reasons to save. The number one reason is to create an emergency fund. Consider the global pandemic that occurred in 2020, that led to millions of job losses and imagine how many people were rendered incapable of sustaining their livelihoods because they lost their jobs or did not have any financial cushion.

Say it with me: **"SAVING IS A LIFE HACK"** because it literally is. If you have not been saving and are ready to build a savings habit, you will need to cut back on some non-essential expenses like the daily Starbucks run, or that midday dessert fix. Five dollars here, Ten dollars there every day will add up.

Think about it, that's Twenty-Five to Fifty dollars a week. Imagine saving that amount on a weekly or bi-weekly basis. You can imagine need to monitor your expenses to effectively establish a saving habit. According to a Bank of America Better Money Habits article, the first step to building a saving habit is to budget for savings, the second step is to record your expenses and review your bills, and the third step is to cut spending.

If you are reading this and thinking, "Well all that sounds like a good fantasy. I do not have the luxury of paying myself," here is a fun fact: 69% of Americans have less than $1,000 in savings, and 45% say they have NO SAVINGS!*(6)*. Considering these two groups, you likely fall into one of these categories if you think saving is a luxury. It is high time that changed. Remember, this book is meant to help you rather than make you feel bad about your current financial situation. The goal is to help you gain clarity on where you are and providing practical tools to get you going. There are many methods to develop the habit of saving; below are three quick and practical ways to cut back on expenses and start saving. Feel free to assess other options available to you.

1. Budget for your savings: Remember in Chapter 1 we discussed your savings goals and creating an emergency fund. By now, you should have established a savings goal (Travel, Housing fund, real estate, e.t.c.). In this step, you need to establish your savings goal amount. This is how much you would like to have saved either by the end of the month or the year. Knowing how much you would like saved by a given time will help you identify how much you need to budget for savings. Essentially, you can easily navigate the terrains of saving once you know where you are headed.

2. Review your bills: There is a chance that you are currently paying more on your Auto insurance, health insurance, Homeowner's/Renter's insurance, phone bill, cable/ streaming services, and even your Auto loan. Yes, you can cut down costs on your auto payment. It's called refinancing (we will discuss this further in another **Moneypoly** series). To keep things simple, let us focus on reviewing your bills here. Compare prices on bills you can afford to and save a few dollars here and there by either switching services and vendors, or by letting go of some monthly subscriptions you do not use (Hulu, Netflix, Amazon, you only need one).

3. Monitor and cut down on spending: When you are going grocery shopping, make a list of exactly what you need rather than going and free styling. You will end up buying whatever pops out to you. Remember, the goal is to purchase exactly what you intended to purchase within your budget.

Let's get into it!

We discussed various types of savings accounts in chapter 2, so feel free to refer to the list and identify which saving instrument you prefer. Once you have identified which type of savings account you would like to open, research your current options, and OPEN IT! Yes, that's right. Put some action to these words and get started now!

Saving Methodologies

So, you have opened your savings account, now it is time to begin to fund the account. After all, it is not a savings account without money saved. First question to ask yourself is, "How am I getting paid?" No, I am not referring to your source of income, but how to get to possess the money. Do you get paid by direct deposit, check or cash? Identifying your means of payment will help in determining the best method of saving for you.

Direct Deposit: You do not receive live checks on pay day, rather, you receive a credit alert as your employer directly deposits the money into your account, hence "direct deposit." If this is how you get paid, you are at a vantage point to start saving. You can save easily without having to think/ do too much; you can automate your savings! Here is how you can do that. Tomorrow, log into your personal compensation profile in your intranet and allocate an amount or a percentage of your check to your newly opened savings account. All you will need are the routing number and account number of your savings account. Set it up the same way you set up your direct deposit. Once you have this set up, you are all set. Savings mode: **ACTIVATED!**

Check: You do receive a check every pay day and you in turn deposit the check in your account either by visiting the ATM or snapping a pic using your bank's mobile app. If you get paid by this means, you can still save. However, it will require additional effort and discipline on your part. You may need to manually deposit these funds or transfer the funds to your savings account.

To set up a recurring transfer, you need to link your checking account to your savings account. If you have a fixed monthly income, you can calculate the amount you would like to deposit every pay period. If you choose the manual approach, you must remember to transfer the funds from your checking account to savings account. If you would like some level of automation, you can set up a recurring transfer in your savings account and auto transfer the same amount every 2 weeks. If you would like to be more aggressive, you can set up an auto transfer on a weekly basis. Savings mode: **ACTIVATED!**

Cash: You receive your compensation in cold cash. It is difficult to expect that there are any legitimate jobs that provide this payment option; however, nothing is impossible. So, with that said, if you receive your payment in cash, you certainly will need to implement a manual process to develop and maintain a savings habit. Especially if you would like to utilize online savings accounts, when you receive the cash on pay day, you head to the bank, deposit the cash into your checking account. Savings mode: **ACTIVATED!**

At this point, you would then transfer funds between your checking and your savings. You can also set up a recurring transfer into your savings account on a weekly or bi-weekly basis; however, you need to ensure that you deposit your cash every pay period without fail or else, you will overdraw your checking account and you will get charged an overdraft fee. This applies to all three payment types, only the risk is lower with direct deposit.

Many banks offer savings accounts but remember the qualifying factors we discussed in chapter 2. The more you vet these accounts, the better. I am a strong proponent of online savings accounts because they offer higher interest rates compared to traditional banks. I would recommend researching current savings accounts, especially online banks to identify the best option for you.

Here is a list of exceptional options as of when this book was written.

 Axos Bank

Ally Bank

Barclays Bank

Marcus By GoldmanSachs

Once you have identified the best saving account for you, you can proceed with a saving methodology above to start saving, then you can put your money to work!

CHAPTER 4

BUDGET

"**O**h no! Not the B word!"

If you are not aware of where each dollar you earn goes, you will quickly realize that your money flies out as quickly as it comes in, if not quicker! Monitoring your spending habits will certainly have a positive impact on your overall financial well-being. As with anything in life, it is critical to pay close attention to and TRACK what is happening to identify whether you are making some progress. For example, for anyone with a goal to lose weight for his/her physical health, he/she tracks caloric intake, workout durations, workout frequency, and the actual weights lost. Budgeting is the same idea, but for financial health.

What is a Budget?

In the words of THE Budgetnista, "A budget is a current picture of what you are doing. It tells you what you can do rather than what you cannot do!" I like how Tiffany Aliche defines a budget because it eliminates the negative conntation and bad rep it has been assigned from years past. From her perspective, this is a positive task with positive results. This tells you what you CAN do; how exciting is that?!

Budgeting can be considered a pseudo income statement for an individual. At the end of the day, we really want a complete picture of income vs. expenses.

We also want to identify whether there are areas where we can reduce or adjust spending habits to keep more money in, which can be churned to savings and then investments!

As introduced to you in Chapter 1, your income is the starting point for budgeting. Without an income, it is difficult to create a budget because all you would have listed on a typical budgeting worksheet would be expenses. This would obviously leave you in the REDZONE (a negative financial state), which we would like to avoid by any means necessary. A legitimate means at least. So, income is important. Say it with me **"Income is important!"**

Before we dive into the technicality of budgeting and how you can get started, I think it is important for you to understand why this is a valuable practice in your MoneyMoves.

Benefits of Budgeting

1. Knowing the source of each Dollar or Pound or Euro.

2. Identifying non-negotiable expenses and highest cost drivers.

3. Knowing the destination of each Dollar or Pound or Euro.

4. Identifying spending habits.

5. Curtailing negative spending habits.

6. Saving more money overall.

Now that we have established an understanding of what a budget is and great reasons to undertake creating a budget, let us proceed with the technical and practical side of budgeting.

Identify your monthly income

To create a budget, you need to first identify your monthly income. I say monthly because it is much more manageable to practice budgeting monthly rather than annually. Referring to the weight loss example, you would not do 300 pushups or burpees on day 1 of your weight loss journey because, well, you have not learned your tolerance level, neither have you built the endurance necessary to successfully complete those pushups or burpees.

So, as we did in Chapter 1, to compute your monthly income you can start by listing all your sources of income. once you have identified each source of income, you can start either with your weekly pay or bi-weekly pay. If you get paid every week, multiply your weekly pay by 4 since there are 4 weeks in a month on average. If you get paid bi-weekly, multiply your bi-weekly paycheck by 2 because you get paid twice in a month.

Identify your monthly expenses

Now that your monthly income is computed, you are ready to identify and list your expenses. Using a monthly expenses worksheet like the worksheet in Chapter 1 when we discussed emergency funds, compute your total monthly expenses.

◆ I have provided a worksheet here for your convenience.

Monthly Expenses
Worksheet

Monthly Expenses	Amount	Percentage
TOTAL (sum):		
Percentage = (amt/total)*100		**%**

Feel free to make a copy of this worksheet if your expense list is longer than the space provided. Also, you can still compute the allocations per expense; this will help you identify your highest cost drivers. Remember to list the seemingly minimal expense.

Note: for expenses that are not consistent monthly, like utilities, cable, hair, rent, e.t.c, you can list these inconsistent expenses are miscellaneous expense. While it is technically not an expense remember to include your monthly savings amount in this list so that you can capture an accurate number for how much you have left after all obligations are met.

All done?

Are you able to identify your highest cost driver? Do you feel the worksheet helped to paint a picture of your current situation? Do you see what you CAN do? Let us unpack that last question, shall we?

After subtracting your total expenses from your total income, are in the GREENZONE or REDZONE?

■■

If you are in the GreenZone, you have some more left over that can be put to great use like paying down/off some debt or investing in your brokerage or retirement account. If you are in the RedZone, then you may need to assess your current expense list and possibly cut out some expenses or adjust vendors for expenses, like insurance or streaming providers. Keep reading for more on how to get to the GreenZone.

To my RedZoner, your next goal is to identify expenses that can either be eliminated or reassessed. Expenses like the daily ritual Starbucks run can be eliminated by you making coffee at home. Imagine saving $5 a day for 12 months. That is 5*5*4*12 = 1,200. That's $1,200 that could be in a high yield savings account that would grow into more by just sitting in the account. That $1,200 can become at least $1,500 by investing it in an ETF or index fund.

So, comb through your expense list and shed the weight! Your greatest MoneyMoves are those you make with a well-informed mind and practical steps.

■■

The technical aspect of budgeting is now taken care of, let us proceed to the practicality of this because without practice, you cannot undertake this a part of your MoneyMoves journey.

To incorporate and practice budgeting, it is helpful to know the different methods of budgeting. According to Erin Lowry, Author of *Broke Millennial: Stop Scraping by and get your financial life together*(7), some budgeting styles include:

1.The Cash Diet: this is the best system for the Spendinista who is not aware of his/her spending habits and needs to rein in his/her expenditures. You would have a set amount of cash in your wallet for the month and once that cash is down to zero, no more spending until the next month!

2. The Envelope System: this system is best for anyone who can put money aside for anticipated expenses beforehand. In this system, you are setting aside funds for each envelope expense category and ensuring that you are not double-crossing envelopes or borrowing from one envelope to fund another.

3. The Track Every Penny System: this system is for anyone who needs to know exactly where money is going. This person must record every. single. transaction to the penny. Personally, this sounds reactive rather than proactive.

4. The Percentage Budgeting: this system is useful for an individual like the income allocation method discussed in chapter 1 where cash on hand is categorized as a percentage of income in 3 sections; Fixed costs, financial goals, and treats or flexible spending funds. Once you have identified these three categories, you can assign a percentage of your choice to each like 50%-30%-20% or 40%-40%-20%.

Remember, the goal of this body of work and financial education is to become a MoverNShaker. That is the profile we are aiming to achieve. Refer to Chapter 2 for more details on characteristics of a MoverNShaker. You can select the budget system that works best for you, but I encourage you to implement the percentage method. After you have identified the percentage of your income that is allocated to the 3 categories, you can set-up your budget accordingly.

Conclusion

If you can take the practical steps outlined in this first edition book, I believe it will create a strong foundation for your transformative MoneyMoves journey! In the next edition of **Monepoly**, we will dive deeper into other ways money can move and work for you. Topics you can look forward to are investing, vehicles of investing, understanding compensation benefits like 401k, IRA, and Health Insurance, and how you can use them to grow your money.

It is critical to note the order in which I am presenting you with financial education information. If you think that you do not need the fundamental information presented in this body of text, I will say think again. Rome was not built in a day, and I am certain it was not built without a foundation. This first edition serves as the foundation for building your financial house and making MoneyMoves!

CITATIONS

1. https://www.suzeorman.com/blog/A-New-Savings-Goal-for-2021

2. https://www.daveramsey.com/blog/how-to-start-investing

3. https://www.businessinsider.com/personal-finance/average-stock-market-return

4. https://www.bankrate.com/personal-finance/debt/aver-age-american-debt/

5. https://www.forbes.com/advisor/banking/types-of-savings-accounts/

6. https://www.fool.com/retirement/2019/12/18/the-percentage-of-americans-with-less-than-1000-in/

7. Lowry, Erin. *Broke Millennial: Stop Scraping by and get your financial life together.* Tarcher Perigee, 2017